Cartoon of Lord (then Captain) Lugard by Spy (Leslie Ward) from *Vanity Fair,* 19th December, 1895. It appeared above the caption "an earnest African".

THE ARCHIVE SERIES

General Editors: C. P. Hill and G. H. Fell

British Imperialism in the Late 19th Century

L. R. Gardiner

Senior Lecturer in History, University of Melbourne

and J. H. Davidson

Junior Lecturer in History, Rhodes University, Grahamstown

Edward Arnold (Publishers) Ltd. London

© L. R. Gardiner and J. H. Davidson 1968
First published 1968

SBN: 7131 1521 1

THE ARCHIVE SERIES

at present contains the following titles:

Disraeli and Conservatism *by* Robin Grinter.
Lenin and the Russian Revolutions *by* F. W. Stacey.
British Imperialism in the Late 19th Century *by* L. R. Gardiner and J. H. Davidson.
The Liberals and the Welfare State *by* R. D. H. Seaman.
Mussolini and the Fascist Era *by* Desmond Gregory.
Hitler and the Rise of the Nazis *by* D. M. Phillips.

Further titles are in preparation.

*Printed in Great Britain by
Cox & Wyman Ltd., London, Reading and Fakenham*

General Preface

The aim of the Archive Series is to provide historical source material suitable for use in secondary schools. Today it is widely and strongly felt to be right to introduce school students of history, in some elementary way, to the raw materials of the subject. The booklets in this series will provide selections of material on historical topics in a form suitable for students of fifteen to seventeen years of age. Each topic has been selected for its interest and importance. The material ranges widely: extracts from newspapers, letters, speeches, diaries, treaties, novels, statutes, and autobiographies are all represented.

Teachers, we imagine, will find the booklets useful in various ways: as a means to enrich a syllabus, as a supplement to textbooks, as the basis for elementary investigation of sources themselves, as illustrations of policies or attitudes, or merely as an occasional change from the normal routine. The series has a uniform format for ease of reference, but the author of each booklet has adopted his own plan of approach. We hope that the series will stimulate interest and increase understanding.

C.P.H.
G.H.F.

Contents

Acknowledgments

Detailed sources for each extract are given at the end of the book. We would also like to thank the following for their permission to reprint copyright material:

A. P. Watt & Son (Extract 21); Mrs George Bambridge and A. P. Watt & Son (Extract 20); The Fabian Society (Extract 8).

Endpapers: Punch Magazine
Cassell and Co. Ltd.

Cover

The final entries in Dr. Livingstone's diary—the last being made on 27th April, 1873, four days before his death. On some days he had strength enough only to write the date, the number of hours travelled etc, but the text of the main entries is as follows:

20th April, Sunday.—Service. Cross over the sponge, Moenda, for food and to be near the headman of these parts, Moanzambamba. I am excessively weak. Village on Moenda sponge, 7 a.m. Cross Lokulu in a canoe. The river is about thirty yards broad, very deep, and flowing in marshes two knots from S.S.E. to N.N.W. into Lake.

21st April.—Tried to ride, but was forced to lie down, and they carried me back to vil. exhausted.

22nd April.—Carried on kitanda over Buga S.W. $2\frac{1}{4}$. [$2\frac{1}{4}$ hours in a south-westerly direction.]

27th April.—Knocked up quite, and remain—recover—sent to buy milch goats. We are on the banks of the Molilamo.

Introduction

In its heyday the British Empire held together a vaster number of territories and peoples than the world had seen. Yet by the end of the First World War, when even more territories were coloured red on the map, the strain was beginning to tell. Today, only a generation after the granting of independence to India and Pakistan, we may well wonder at the speed of its dissolution. The United Nations has admitted over a score of former British territories to membership, a process still continuing. Britain herself has yet to work out fully the implications of losing an empire.

These facts are important because they show how close we are to the men and the events represented in this selection of documents. 'Colonialism' and 'imperialism' are among the dirtiest words in international politics today, and in reading some of these documents we may come to see why. Other documents here should, however, dispel some of the sense of embarrassment which now hangs heavily around everything associated with Britain's imperial past.

The British practice of allowing government archives to be inspected after fifty (now changed to thirty) years has also delivered British Imperialism into the hands of scholars. They are beginning to present the subject with fuller knowledge and greater detachment. This introduction is no place to embark on a summary of recently reconsidered verdicts. It is sufficient to insist that British Imperialism was neither as chaste as some defenders supposed nor as coarse as some critics have claimed. There was unselfish aspiration, sacrificial endeavour, statesmanship, strong sense of duty and sheer hard work together with unscrupulous adventuring, including bullying and greed, much noisy and distasteful patriotism, a touch of hypocrisy and some dangerous delusion—in short a characteristic human activity when many individuals are caught up in a mass movement. It was always so, and one of the rewards of a study of the past is to become acquainted with the best and the worst of what men can do. In this way we may be saved from despair and yet face life with no illusions about the beast within ourselves.

This booklet presents a selection of documents about some of the strongest strands which were woven into the Imperial banner.

Each strand is distinct; none is separate. In the minds and activities of Empire builders whether in the field, at the desk or in the armchair there were always several strands entangled. British destiny, British racial superiority, British civilizing mission to the world, British economic advantage, the unity of British peoples everywhere, British world peace, the rescue of the British poor from degradation: all these and others fitted into a pattern. More truly there were many patterns; almost as many patterns as there were British Imperialists.

To understand what was thought and done in the name of British Imperialism we should try to recapture the mood of those who took part in the movement. The best way is to listen to their voices. This is often difficult. To hear now dead persons positively maintaining, say, a great destiny for 'the British race' is to listen to what seems a mixture of arrogance, delusion and hypocrisy. Our own strong convictions will be different but they also may astonish future generations.

As we arrange the thoughts and actions of what is hardly more than one generation of Imperialists our classification must be somewhat arbitrary. The careful reader may well prefer to place any of the documents in a different section. Some of our documents about Processes (Section 6), for example, could be included under Jingoism (Section 2).

What we have done is to illustrate the variety in British Imperial activity from about 1860 to 1902. For this reason we have not arranged the documents in chronological order. Instead we have divided the material into *Promptings of Empire* and into *Machinery of Empire;* that is between the conceptions, such as they were, and the execution, such as it was.

It is often assumed that late nineteenth-century Britain was almost totally committed to Imperialism. This is wrong. British opposition to Imperialism could easily occupy a large part of any study of British Imperialism. For this reason we have sought to include some of the critical views expressed, and have placed them alongside the opinions from which they strongly dissented. These dissenting views are marked with an asterisk.

A. Promptings of Empire

SECTION 1.

INTELLECTUAL: DESTINY OF RACE, ENGLISH CIVILIZATION, SERVICE OF MAN

In this section we examine the foundations of the late nineteenth-century Englishman's supreme sense of confidence.

The first extract from Trollope is typical of the fashionable view held in the 1850s and 1860s that England ought to abandon her colonies. Yet Trollope adds something new, an awareness of England's mission. Dilke (No. 3) sets the tone for our period by turning Trollope upside down. Since England must spread English government and institutions amongst native peoples she must control them. Johnston (No. 4) illustrates this by showing how the Negro is improved immeasurably by British rule, while Froude (No. 5) shows the strength of English institutions (and hence their validity) by the ease with which they are transplanted. To go from Froude to Milner (No. 6) is a jump indeed: here is British racism stated in most uncompromising terms.

The next two extracts are removed from the main stream of thought we have just outlined but their interest lies in the degree to which they have absorbed it. Bonwick (No. 7) in expressing anxiety for the native races uses the language of Charles Darwin, whose views on evolution were rapidly misapplied in international affairs to explain the superiority of one power over another. Something of this can be seen in the final extract in which Bernard Shaw argues against the Boers of South Africa and for British control because of Britain's political maturity and greater sense of responsibility.

1. *Anthony Trollope (1815–1882), author of* Barchester Towers, *spent most of his life as a Post Office official, inventing the common letter box as well as writing his fifty novels. He also travelled extensively throughout the colonies. This extract is from* The West Indies *(1859), one of his four travel books.*

The present position and prospects of the children of Great Britain are sufficiently noble, and sufficiently extended. One need not begrudge to others their limited share in the population and government of the world's welfare. While so large a part of North America and Australia remain still savage—waiting the white man's foot—waiting, in fact, for the foot of the Englishman, there can be no reason why we should doom our children to swelter and grow pale within the tropics. A certain work has been ours to do there, a certain amount of remaining work it is still probably our lot to complete. But when that is done; when civilization, commerce, and education shall have been spread; when sufficient of our blood shall have been infused into the veins of those children of the sun; then, I think, we may be ready, without stain to our patriotism, to take off our hats and bid farewell to the West Indies. . . .

We have risen so high that we may almost boast to have placed ourselves above national glory. The welfare of the coming world is now the proper care of the Anglo Saxon race.

2. *This second Trollope extract is from a newsletter for* The Liverpool Mercury *written from Sydney in 1875. The recent killing of Commodore Goodenough in the Solomon Islands leads him to reflect on British colonial policy.*

. . . England had lost one of her best seamen—a man tender as he was brave, a man of science, full of the highest aspirations, fit for any great work—such a one as no nation can afford to lose lightly.

And now the question recurs with which I began this letter—what are we to do with the South Sea Islands? There will probably be a strong feeling at home that, because one of our great officers has been murdered in the execution of his duty, some vengeance should be taken; and yet can we fairly say that these islanders were to blame, acting as they did according to their lights? . . .

It is certain that we do not mean to take possession of those lands for our own purposes—as we have done in Australia and New Zealand, in which though our coming has exterminated, or will soon exterminate, the natives, even so sad a result as that is justified to our consciences by the opening of new homes to men of higher races. If we had all the islands lying within the tropics we could not find in them a fitting domicile for a single working European. If we look round the world within the tropics we must come to that conclusion as to the centre belt. And certainly we do not want an extended dominion over black subjects. The missionary tells us we may make Christians of them. I will not contradict the missionary, whose work is entitled to our loving respect. But I cannot but see that hitherto his success has hardly been sufficient to justify the assistance of our ships of war. At present it seems that we do not quite know what to do, and that we drift into the possessions of undesirable so-called colonies.

3. *Sir Charles Dilke (1843–1911) made an early and immediate impact with his book* Greater Britain *in 1868. Dilke, a powerful advocate of Imperialism, became a prominent politician before he was accused of adultery. The case against him failed but it was enough to ruin the career of a potentially great statesman.*

In 1866 and 1867, I followed England round the world: everywhere I was in English-speaking, or in English-governed lands. If I remarked [noticed] that climate, soil, manners of life, that mixture with other peoples had modified the blood, I saw, too, that in essentials the race was always one.

The idea which in all the length of my travels has been at once my fellow and my guide—a key wherewith to unlock the hidden things of strange new lands—is a conception, however imperfect, of the grandeur of our race, already girdling the earth, which it is destined, perhaps, eventually to overspread.

In America, the peoples of the world are being fused together, but they are run into an English mould: Alfred's laws and Chaucer's tongue are theirs whether they would or no. There are men who say that Britain in her age will claim the glory of having planted greater Englands across the seas. They fail to perceive that she has done more than found plantations of her own—that she has imposed her institutions upon the offshoots of Germany, of Ireland, of Scandinavia, and of Spain. Through America England is speaking to the world. . . .

Sketches of Saxondom may be of interest even upon humbler grounds: the development of the England of Elizabeth is to be found, not in the Britain of Victoria, but in half the habitable globe. If two small islands are by courtesy styled 'Great', America, Australia, India, must form a Greater Britain.

In America we have seen the struggles of the dear races against the cheap—the endeavours of the English to hold their own against the Irish and the Chinese. In New Zealand, we found the stronger and more energetic race pushing from the earth the shrewd and laborious descendants of the Asian Malays; in Australia, the English triumphant, and the cheaper races excluded from the soil not by distance merely, but by arbitrary legislation; in India, we saw the solution of the problem of the officering of the cheaper by the dearer race. Everywhere we have found that the difficulties which impede the progress to universal dominion of the English people lie in the conflict with the cheaper races. The result of our survey is such as to give us reason for the belief that race distinctions will long continue, that miscegenation will go but little way towards blending races; that the dearer are, on the whole, likely to destroy the cheaper peoples, and that Saxondom will rise triumphant from the doubtful struggle.

4. *Sir Harry Johnston (1858–1927) a leading painter, natural scientist, explorer, diplomat and administrator began his African career in 1876. He coined the phrase 'Cape-to-Cairo' yet he knew only too well that Empire meant not flag-waving but hard work amongst Africans. He writes here in the* Fortnightly Review *1890.*

By their own unaided efforts I doubt whether the Negroes would ever advance much above the status of savagery in which they still exist in those parts of Africa where neither European nor Arab civilization has as yet reached them. There they are still to be found leading a life which, in its essential features of culture and social organization, is scarcely altered from what it was four thousand years ago, when the black men and their simple arts and savage surroundings were truthfully limned in Egyptian frescoes. The Negro seems to require the intervention of some superior race before he can be roused to any definite advance from the low stage of human development in which he has contentedly remained for many thousand years. But, when once he does come in contact with civilization, he accepts it with extraordinary readiness, and surpasses all other low-grade varieties of man in the facility with which in one generation, in the one individual, he can skip two or three thousand years, and transform himself from a naked, brutish savage into an excellent shorthand clerk, a telegraph operator, a skilled photographer, a steamer-engineer, a first-class cook, or an irreproachable butler. The black race has, of course, like the other sections of humanity, many faults and shortcomings. It is, as a rule, strongly averse to continuous, regularized hard work, and its average disposition is passionate, noisy, vain and quarrelsome. But with all his defects the Negro is more likeable, more akin to us of the white race in disposition, and far less alien to our civilization than is the cold, inscrutable, reptilian Chinese. In the course of two or three centuries I believe the Negroes of British Africa will only differ from their white fellow-subjects in the colour of their skins. . . .

5. *The historian James Anthony Froude (1818–94) was among the first to awaken interest in the colonies. He saw their value mainly as a field for emigration and he visited most of them. In this extract from* Oceana *(1886) he waxes eloquent about Ercildoun, a large property near Ballarat in Victoria. The house still stands and is still occupied.*

We had left Melbourne early and it was not yet noon. We were to sleep at Ballarat, but were not immediately to stop there; we were engaged to a luncheon party at a squatter's station, twenty miles beyond, from which we were to return in the evening. We have all heard of squatters' stations. We imagine (at least I did) a wild tract of forest, a great pastoral range, a wooden hut run up in the middle of it; men, dogs, horses, cattle, semi-savage all; bushrangers perhaps skulking not far off; the native and naked blacks of the soil retiring slowly before advancing civilization and hovering on the white man's skirts; and for the rest the rude hospitality of nomad settlers amid a life like that of the ancient Scythians. This is what I looked for when I was told that I was to be taken to a squatter's station, and the reality was again unlike the anticipation. . . .

We came at last to a gate, which needed only a lodge to be like the entrance to a great English domain. . . . After passing a second gate we found more variety. There were plantations which had been skilfully made. English trees were mixed with the indigenous. . . . A third gate and we were between high trimmed hedges of evergreen, catching a sight at intervals of a sheet of water overhung with weeping willows; a moment more, and we were at the door of what might have been an ancient Scotch manor house, solidly built of rough-hewn granite, the walls overrun with ivy, climbing roses, and other multitudinous creepers, which formed a border to the diamond-paned, old-fashioned windows. On the north side was a clean-mown and carefully-watered lawn, with tennis-ground and croquet-ground, flowerbeds bright with scarlet geraniums, heliotropes, verbenas, fuchsias—we had arrived, in fact, at an English aristocrat's country house reproduced in another hemisphere, and shone upon at night by other constellations. Inside, the illusion was even more complete. . . . .

We found a high-bred English family—English in everything except that they were Australian-born, and cultivated perhaps above the English average. . . . Good pictures hung round the rooms. Books, reviews, newspapers—all English—and the 'latest publications' were strewed about the tables—the *Saturday*, the *Spectator*, and the rest of them. The contrast between the scene which I had expected and the scene which I found took my breath away. . . .

It was a day to be remembered, and a scene to be remembered. Here was not England only, but old-fashioned baronial England, renewing itself spontaneously in a land of gold and diggers, a land which in my own recollection was a convict drain, which we have regarded since as a refuge for the waifs and strays of our superfluous population for whom we can find no use at home. These were the people whom our proud legislature thought scarcely to be worth the trouble of preserving as our fellow-subjects. It seemed to me as if at no distant time the condescension might be on the other side. . . .

6. *Viscount Milner (1854–1925) was a dominating and perhaps the most domineering British overseas ruler or proconsul. After his death this statement of Imperial belief was found among his papers. He had expressed similar views when he stood, unsuccessfully, for Parliament in 1885. Once he made up his mind Milner never changed.*

CREDO. Key to my position.

I am a Nationalist and not a cosmopolitan . . . I am a British (indeed primarily an English) Nationalist. If I am also an Imperialist, it is because the destiny of the English race, owing to its insular position and long supremacy at sea, has been to strike fresh roots in different parts of the world. My patriotism knows no geographical but only racial limits. I am an Imperialist and not a Little Englander, because I am a British Race Patriot. . . . The British State must follow the race, must comprehend it wherever it settles in appreciable numbers as an independent community. If the swarms constantly being thrown off by the parent hive are lost to the State, the State is irreparably weakened. We cannot afford to part with so much of our best blood. We have already parted with much of it, to form the nucleus of another wholly separate though fortunately friendly State. We cannot suffer a repetition of the process.

*7. *James Bonwick (1817–1906), author of* The Lost Tasmanian Race *and one of the first of Australia's historians, was an Englishman, who lived in Tasmania and Victoria. He returned in 1870. The last Tasmanian aboriginal died in 1876.*

PREFACE

Another edition being called for, the Author declined the re-production of the *Last of the Tasmanians*, an expensive work, and preferred, for the popularization of views favouring the claims of Aborigines, to produce, in a simpler form, the leading facts of that sad tale of a Colonial Past. Such is the narrative given in *The Lost Tasmanian Race*.

Of late years, great disturbances have occurred in the relations of Whites and Coloured peoples. Zulus, Indians, Bechuanas, Malagasy, Annamese, Australians, Pacific Islanders, Egyptians and Soudanese, have trembled before the might of European civilization. This has been a terrible period of anxiety to all Coloured nations.

Are all *Dark Skins* to perish, like the unhappy Tasmanians, before Europeans? Have we not often been, in our civilizing processes, more savage than the Savages?

If the Natural *Law of Selection* necessitates the destruction of inferior races, as History has illustrated thus far, is there not in Humanity a *Higher Law*, happily better recognized in our day, which should and could be employed, by moral force, to resist this fearfully selfish struggle for existence?

Perhaps, in this Colonial record, replies appear to some of these deeply interesting inquiries.

It is, at any rate, hoped that the perusal of these pages may raise up a few more friends for poor Aborigines.
Sutton, Surrey.
April 17th, 1884.

8. *George Bernard Shaw (1856–1950) the dramatist, was an active Socialist. He compiled the tract* Fabianism and the Empire *(1900), which suggested that, for want of something better, Britain should rule in South Africa in the interest of the world community.*

... a Great Power, consciously or unconsciously, must govern in the interests of civilization as a whole; and it is not to those interests that such mighty forces as gold-fields, and the formidable armaments that can be built upon them, should be wielded irresponsibly by small communities of frontiersmen. Theoretically they should be internationalized, not British Imperialized; but until the Federation of the World becomes an accomplished fact, we must accept the most responsible Imperial federations available as a substitute for it. ...

QUESTIONS:
1. Why was it claimed that the British were superior to others?
2. What similarities were there between the views of Trollope, Dilke and Johnston towards Afro-Asian peoples?
3. What are the similarities and differences between the two Trollope extracts? Why have his attacks on British occupation of the tropics become much sharper?
4. What do we learn from Froude about an Englishman's expectations of settlement colonies such as Australia?
5. How does Bonwick differ from opinions expressed in other extracts in this Section?

SECTION 2

POLITICAL: STATESMEN'S CLAIMS AND JINGOISM

With Disraeli's 1872 Crystal Palace speech (No. 9)· the ideas of Section 1 entered practical politics. Disraeli established the Conservatives as Imperialists and successfully labelled the Liberals as anti-imperialists. Not least among his converts was the Queen (No. 11).

During Disraeli's Conservative government (1874–80) the word Jingo was first used in a music hall song of 1877 to mean patriotism run wild.

> 'We don't want to fight
> But by Jingo, if we do
> We've got the ships
> We've got the men
> We've got the money too!'

Hobson (No. 13) denounced such music hall Imperialism. Others like Inglis (No. 12) in India shouted an appalling Jingoist view, as did some school text books (No. 30). In contrast Curzon nobly called upon Indians and British to co-operate in creating a new Imperial India (No. 10).

9. *Benjamin Disraeli (1804–81) quickly reacted to powerful British political opinion. He sensed the rising interest in Imperialism in 1872 and did much to further the movement when Prime Minister, 1874–80.*

If you look to the history of this country since the advent of Liberalism—forty years ago [i.e. since the 1832 Reform Act]—you will find that there has been no effort so continuous, so subtle, supported by so much energy, and carried on with so much ability and acumen, as the attempts of Liberalism to effect the disintegration of the Empire of England. . . . .

Well, what has been the result of this attempt during the reign of Liberalism for the disintegration of the Empire? It has entirely failed. But how has it failed? Through the sympathy of the Colonies for the Mother Country. They have decided that the Empire shall not be destroyed; and in my opinion no Minister in this country will do his duty who neglects any opportunity of reconstructing as much as possible our Colonial Empire, and of responding to those distant sympathies which may become the source of incalculable strength and happiness to this land. . . .

The issue is not a mean one. It is whether you will be content to be a comfortable England, modelled and moulded upon Continental principles and meeting in due course an inevitable fate, or whether you will be a great country, an Imperial country, a country where your sons, when they rise, rise to paramount positions, and obtain not merely the esteem of their countrymen, but command the respect of the world.

10 *The Marquess Curzon of Kedlestone (1859–1925) was fascinated by the East, through which he travelled extensively. He was never one for the 'sordid policy of self-effacement' and his term as Viceroy (1898–1905) is usually recognized as the zenith of British rule in India. This speech to the Convocation of Calcutta University in 1902 shows Curzon's vision undimmed by the disappointments of the later years of his government.*

And now to all of you together let me address these concluding words. The spirit of nationality is moving in the world, and it is an increasing force in the lives and ideals of men. Founded upon race, and often cemented by language and religion, it makes small nations great, and great nations greater. It teaches men how to live, and, in emergencies, it teaches them how to die. But, for its full realization, a spirit of unity, and not of disintegration, is required. There must be a sacrifice of the smaller to the larger interest, and a subordination of the unit to the system. In India it should not be a question of India for the Hindus, or India for the Musulmans, or descending to minor fractions, of Bengal for the Bengalis, or the Deccan for the Mahratta Brahmans. That would be a retrograde and dissolvent process. Neither can it be India for the Indians alone. The last two centuries during which the British have been in this country cannot be wiped out. They have profoundly affected the whole structure of national thought and existence. They have quickened the atrophied veins of the East and the life-blood of the West. They have modified old ideas and created new ones. . . .

Out of this intermingling of the East and the West, a new patriotism, and a more refined and cosmopolitan sense of nationality, are emerging. It is one in which the Englishman may share with the Indian, for he has helped to create it, and in which the Indian may share with the Englishman, since it is their common glory. When an Englishman says that he is proud of India, it is not of battlefields and sieges, nor of exploits in the Council Chamber or at the desk that he is principally thinking. He sees the rising standards of intelligence, of moral conduct, of comfort and prosperity, among the Native peoples, and he rejoices in their advancement. Similarly, when an Indian says that he is proud of

India, it would be absurd for him to banish from his mind all that has been, and is being, done for the resuscitation of his country by the alien race to whom have been committed its destinies. Both are tillers in the same field, and both are concerned in the harvest. From their joint labours it is that this new and composite patriotism is springing into life. It is Asian, for its roots are embedded in the traditions and the aspirations of an Eastern people; and it is European, because it is aglow with the illumination of the West. In it are summed up all the best hopes for the future of this country, both for your race and for mine. We are ordained to walk here in the same track together for many a long day to come. You cannot do without us. We should be impotent without you. Let the Englishman and the Indian accept the consecration of a union that is so mysterious as to have in it something of the divine, and let our common ideal be a united country and a happier people. (Loud and continued cheers).

11. *Queen Victoria who insisted on being fully consulted about Government policy, expressed strong but commonplace opinions about almost everything. She was boisterously patriotic in welcoming a ready defence and an eager extension of British influence overseas.*

The first extract shows her views on the need for British occupation of Egypt, which she pressed on her reluctant Prime Minister, Gladstone. Egyptian national revolt threatened British investments and control of the Suez Canal, the vital link between Britain and India.

Queen Victoria to Earl Granville (Foreign Secretary) Confidential.

Balmoral Castle, October 22nd, 1883: ... As regards *Egypt* and the Troops, the Queen will not give her consent to their *withdrawal* from Egypt, as the interests of Egypt as well as of this country require their remaining. She believes many, if not most, of his colleagues will agree in this; but she fears Mr. Gladstone and Lord Hartington [the War Secretary] are inclined to be *weak upon it.* The Egyptians cannot govern themselves, that *everyone says* who is not inclined to yield to the cry of *non-interference* in *everything.* This must be met by an *honest* firm answer that it is imposible to say *when* the British troops *can* go, in the interest of Egypt and of this country.

We have not allowed precious British blood to be shed only to see Egypt fall into the hands of France and Italy.

During the French conquest of Madagascar in 1883 an English missionary was unjustly imprisoned. The French Government dismissed the chief officer responsible and paid the missionary £1,000 compensation. Queen Victoria was displeased.

Queen Victoria to Mr. Gladstone.
Balmoral, October 30th, 1883: . . . As regards Madagascar and the insufficiency of the reparation the Queen has telegraphed what she has meant. What she fears is a growing tendency to swallow insults and affronts and not taking them up in that high tone which they used formerly to be, and which is so much the case in private transactions now-a-days.

Insults to the honour of men and women, slander and defamation of character since duelling (a thing in itself not to be defended but which still kept up a high tone) has ceased, are not resented or put down as a proper sense of chivalrous honour would demand them to be. This is an increasing evil which should carefully be watched.

12. *James Inglis, a Scot with considerable experience throughout the Empire, lived in India, New Zealand and in New South Wales where he was Minister for Public Instruction in the Parkes Government of 1887–89. He comments here on India.*

All educated respectable Europeans with a stake in the country should be made Justices of the Peace, with limited powers to try petty cases. There is a vast material—loyalty, educated minds, an honest desire to do justice, independence, and a genuine scorn of everything pettifogging and underhand—that the Indian Government would do well to utilize. The best friend of the Baboo cannot acquit him of a tendency to temporize, a hankering after finesse, a too fatal facility to fall under pecuniary temptation. The educated gentleman planter of the present day is above suspicion, and before showering titles and honours on native gentlemen, elevating them to the bench, and deluging the services with them, it might be worth our rulers' while to utilize, or try to utilize, the experience, loyalty, honour, and integrity of those of our countrymen who might be willing to place their services at the disposal of Government. 'India for the Indians' is a very good cry; it sounds well; but it will not do to push it to its logical issue. Unless Indians can govern India wisely and well, in accordance with modern national ideas, they have no more right to India than Hottentots have to the Cape, or the black fellows to Australia. In my opinion, Hindoos would never govern Hindostan half, quarter, nay, one tithe as well as Englishmen. Make more of your Englishmen in India then, make not less of your Baboo if you please, but make more of your Englishmen. Keep them loyal and content. Treat them kindly and liberally. One Englishman contented, loyal, and industrious in an Indian district, is a greater pillar of strength to the Indian Government than ten dozen Baboos or Zemindars, let them have as many titles, decorations, university degrees or certificates of loyalty from junior civilians as they may. Not India for the Indians, but India for Imperial Britain say I.

*13. *J. A. Hobson (1858–1940) wrote* The Psychology of Jingoism (1901) *during the Boer War which he vigorously opposed. Hobson recognized the music hall as a transmitter of crude emotions. Lord Salisbury had already suggested that the popular and Imperialist newspaper, the* Daily Mail, *founded in 1896, appealed to those who read but could not think.*

A gradual debasement of popular art attending the new industrial era of congested, ugly, manufacturing towns has raised up the music-hall to be the most powerful instrument of such musical and literary culture as the people are open to receive.

Among large sections of the middle and the labouring classes, the music-hall, and the recreative public-house into which it shades off by imperceptible degrees, are a more potent educator than the church, the school, the political meeting, or even the press. Into this 'lighter self' of the city populace the artiste conveys by song or recitation crude notions upon morals and politics, appealing by coarse humour or exaggerated pathos to the animal lusts of an audience stimulated by alcohol into appreciative hilarity.

In ordinary times politics plays no important part in these feasts of sensationalism, but the glorification of brute force and an ignorant contempt for foreigners are ever-present factors which at great political crises make the music-hall a very serviceable engine for generating military passion. The art of the music-hall is the only 'popular' art of the present day. . . . The neurotic temperament generated by town life seeks natural relief in stormy sensational appeals, and the crowded life of the streets, or other public gatherings, give the best medium for communicating them. This is the very atmosphere of Jingoism . . . Jingoism is the passion of the spectator, the inciter, the backer, not of the fighter; it is a collective or mob passion. . . .

QUESTIONS:
1. Why was it easy and perhaps natural for people such as Queen Victoria and Inglis to be Jingos?
2. Was Disraeli's charge against the Liberals convincing?
3. Why was Curzon such a devout believer in the Indian Empire?
4. How does Hobson show the music halls to be an instrument of Imperialism?

SECTION 3

ECONOMIC AND SOCIAL

The economic motive for Imperialism was stated more bluntly in the 1890s as other nations overtook British industrial output and sheltered their markets behind protective tariffs. In 1893 the Foreign Secretary was busy 'pegging out claims for the future' (No. 14). Philanthropy aside, Africa must be developed—there lay the markets that British industry sorely needed (Lugard, No. 15). The only way to guarantee those markets, as Mary Kingsley pointed out, was by annexation.

Chamberlain held that British working men's wages depended on the prosperity of the home industries which served Empire markets. The working man must therefore support Imperialism. Hobson argued against this. It was the gross inequality of wealth in Britain which made rich men invest in overseas markets. Improve conditions at home and there the necessary new markets would be found. Rhodes, with characteristic directness, at once saw the danger of the poor but adapted it to his own ambitions of peopling Rhodesia.

14. *The Earl of Rosebery (1847–1929) described himself as a 'Liberal Imperialist'. He was a forceful and popular speaker and was Prime Minister 1894–95. In 1894 he made history as the first Prime Minister in office to win the Derby.*

There are two schools who view with some apprehension the growth of our Empire. The first is composed of those nations who, coming somewhat late into the field, find that Great Britain has some of the best plots already marked out. To those nations I will say that they must remember that our colonies were taken— to use a well-known expression—at prairie value, and that we have made them what they are. We may claim that whatever lands other nations may have touched and rejected and we have culti- vated and improved are fairly parts of our Empire, which we may claim to possess by an indisputable title. But there is another ground on which the extension of our Empire is greatly attacked, and the attack comes from a quarter nearer home. It is said that our Empire is already large enough and does not need extension. That would be true enough if the world were elastic, but, un- fortunately, it is not elastic, and we are engaged at the present moment, in the language of mining, in 'pegging out claims for the the future'. We have to consider not what we want now, but what we shall want in the future. We have to consider what countries must be developed either by ourselves or some other nation, and we have to remember that it is part of our responsibility and heritage to take care that the world, as far as it can be moulded by us, shall receive the Anglo-Saxon and not another character. . . .

15. *Sir Frederick, later first Baron, Lugard (1858–1945) was an active soldier in colonial wars 1878–87. He then served as an agent of British trading companies in tropical Africa. Forceful and able, he became the indispensable servant of the Royal Niger Company and then of British government in Nigeria, which he dominated 1912–19. Lugard, a splendid administrator, a great realist, never forgot that in a colonial situation both sides should profit. He shows here the need for Imperial trade to bolster the British economy as well as concern for African welfare.*

(*a*) Let us admit that commercial enterprise in Africa is under- taken for our own benefit, as much as and more than for the benefit of the African. We have spoken already of the vital necessity of new markets for the Old World. It is, therefore, to our very obvious advantage to teach the millions of Africa the wants of civilization, so that whilst supplying them we may receive in return the pro- ducts of their country and the labour of their hands. It is assuredly a noble and praiseworthy result that we should introduce decency and sanitation, even though it be by the medium of Manchester cottons and Pears' soap, but there is . . . an even more substantial benefit which we can confer upon the African in return for his produce and his labour. That benefit consists of effective adminis-tration, by which security to life and property is assured to the humblest native, and the carnage of the raiding tribes and the onslaught of the slaver become things of the past; by which the smallpox and the pestilence, which today decimate the population, and the cattle disease, and possibly the locust pest, which deprive him of his food and leave him to die of starvation, yield to scientific methods and to sanitation. It is to our commercial advantage to teach the native that our presence is for his good, and to educate him to desire those amenities of civilization which are more broadly expressed in bales of cottons and boxes of hardware. It matters not to discuss the academic question of whether the Negro is happier dancing stark naked under the moon, or eating pumpkin in the sun, as Carlyle described him. We want him clothed because our looms will clothe him; we want him housed and ornamented because our Sheffield firms will supply the wherewithal. We want his fields to double their produce, and that produce to be of a marketable quality, because it is needed by our manufacturers here in England. We deal today with the commer-cial side of the question: the 'philanthropic dividends' we will put aside for the moment; they are concomitants.

(*b*) How greatly our home iron and steel industries need a stimulus may be gauged by the facts and figures quoted by an able writer in *The Times* of the 15th of August [1895]. 'There has not only been an absence of actual progress,' he says, 'but in not a few departments there has been a more or less considerable amount of retrogression; whereas the average value of our iron and steel exports for the four years ended 1883 was about £2,900,000, the average for the four years ended 1894 was only £2,200,000. Our iron and steel manufacturers in the interval found it increasingly difficult to retain such hold as they had obtained in the principal markets of the world, and new markets were occupied by others with a promptness and avidity that were really startling. Even our colonial markets seemed to disappear from our grasp. A very little inquiry showed that Germany and Belgium had largely occupied the markets in which British manu-facturers formerly deemed themselves to be supreme and un-challenged. And not only were our colonial and foreign markets invaded, but we found that even our home market was gradually yielding to the sustained pressure of foreign competition. Profits dwindled and declined on every hand, and not a few works were closed entirely.'

16. *Mary Kingsley (1862–1900) realized that African society could not keep out Europeans and that in West Africa traders would not continue to profit without further British annexation.*

I think trade is the most important thing in West Africa. .... It seems to me that to set about developing the natural resources of our possessions and not to trouble our heads about getting more territory, as a certain class of politicians are fond of advising us to do, is like getting expensive furniture into a house that has no roof on it; for the internal resources of our possessions [on coastal West Africa] mainly consist of malaria, mud and mangroves. The trade articles—rubber, ivory and palm oil—that come up in great quantities from our possessions is all trade from the interior. Were it not for the Royal Niger Company who have done and are doing a work of which every Englishman should feel proud, our position as regards opening up and exploiting the interior would be a very despicable one; for where outside outside the Company can you find Englishmen worthy to be named as explorers in the same breath with de Brazza, Binger and Dr. Zintgraff? I am told the present value of our coastal possessions is between three and four millions sterling annually. It will not be that long if we do not possess ourselves of the interior trade routes. ....

17. *Joseph Chamberlain (1836–1914), a Birmingham manufacturer, was keenly interested in British overseas trade and in the contentment of city workers. When he later became Colonial Secretary in 1895 he did not forget these interests. In this Birmingham speech in 1894 he combined them.*

.... in order that we may have more employment to give we must create more demand. [Hear, hear] Give me the demand for more goods and then I will undertake to give plenty of employment in making the goods; and the only thing, in my opinion, that the Government can do in order to meet this great difficulty that we are considering, is so to arrange its policy that every inducement shall be given to the demand; that new markets shall be created, and that old markets shall be effectually developed. [Cheers]

You are aware that some of my opponents please themselves occasionally by finding names for me—[Laughter]—and among other names lately they have been calling me a Jingo. [Laughter]

I am no more a Jingo than you are. [Hear, hear] But for the reasons and arguments I have put before you tonight I am convinced that it is a necessity as well as a duty for us to uphold the dominion and empire which we now possess. [Loud cheers] For these reasons, among others, I would never lose the hold which we now have over our great Indian dependency—[Hear, hear]—by far the greatest and most valuable of all the customers we have or ever shall have in this country. For the same reasons I approve of the continued occupation of Egypt, and for the same reasons I have urged upon this Government and upon previous Governments, the necessity for using every legitimate opportunity to extend our influence and control in that great African continent which is now being opened up to civilization and to commerce; and, lastly, it is for the same reasons that I hold that our navy should be strengthened—[loud cheers]—until its supremacy is so assured that we cannot be shaken in any one of the possessions which we hold or may hold hereafter.

Believe me, if in any one of the places to which I have referred any change took place which deprived us of that control and influence of which I have been speaking, the first to suffer would be the working men of this country. Then indeed, we should see a distress which would not be temporary, but which would be chronic, and we should find that England was entirely unable to support the enormous population which is now maintained by the aid of her foreign trade. If the working men of this country ... understand their own interests, they will never lend any countenance to the doctrines of those politicians who never lose an opportunity of pouring contempt and abuse upon the brave Englishmen, who, even at this moment, in all parts of the world are carving out new dominions for Britain, and are opening up fresh markets for British commerce and laying out fresh fields for British Labour. [Applause]

18. *Cecil Rhodes (1853–1902), founder of Rhodesia, dreamed of an all-British Africa link stretching from Cape to Cairo. As an arch-Imperialist, his recipe of 1895 for avoiding revolution at home is best known through this disapproving quotation in Lenin's* Imperialism: The Highest Stage of Capitalism (*1917*).

I was in the East End of London (workers' section) yesterday and attended a meeting of unemployed. I listened to the wild speeches, which were just a cry for 'bread,' 'bread', 'bread', and on my way home I pondered over the scene and I became more than ever convinced of the importance of imperialism. ... My cherished idea is a solution for the social problem, i.e. in order to save the 40,000,000 inhabitants of the United Kingdom from a bloody civil war, we colonial statesmen must acquire new lands for settling the surplus population, to provide new markets for the goods produced in the factories and mines. The Empire, as I have always said, is a bread and butter question. If you want to avoid civil war, you must become imperialists.

*19. *J. A. Hobson's* Imperialism (*1902*) *established a connection between capitalism and the pursuit of Empire. The English poor could not buy much. English investors therefore turned overseas, and increasingly to colonial markets controlled by Britain. This to Hobson was to neglect the poor and to seek imaginary profits. The influence of this first systematized assault on Imperialism continues today when Afro-Asians attack 'neo-colonialism'.*

A nation may either, following the example of Denmark or Switzerland, put brains into agriculture, develop a finely varied system of public education, general and technical, apply the ripest science to its special manufacturing industries, and so support in progressive comfort and character a considerable population upon a strictly limited area; or it may, like Great Britain, neglect its agriculture, allowing its lands to go out of cultivation and its population to grow up in towns, fall behind other nations in its methods of education and in the capacity of adapting to its uses the latest scientific knowledge, in order that it may squander its pecuniary and military resources in forcing bad markets and finding speculative fields of investment in distant corners of the earth, adding millions of square miles and of unassimilable population to the area of the Empire.

The driving forces of class interest which stimulate and support this false economy we have explained. No remedy will serve which permits the future operation of these forces.

It is idle to attack Imperialism or Militarism as political expedients or policies unless the axe is laid at the root of the tree, and the classes for whose interest Imperialism works are shorn of the surplus revenues which seek this outlet.

QUESTIONS:

1. Why were Liberals usually suspicious of British Imperialism?
   Why was Lord Rosebery, a Liberal politician, a supporter of British expansion?
   In what ways did Rosebery's views agree with those of Conservative upholders of Empire?
2. What do you consider to be the key sentence in Lugard's statement in document 15*a*? Give reasons.
3. How does Lugard's view of the nature of the African (No. 15*a*) differ from Johnston's (No. 4)?
4. Why did some writers think that African trade was not enough, but that African territory itself should be taken over by Britain?
5. What interest, according to Chamberlain and Rhodes, were working class people supposed to have in the Empire?
6. What, according to Hobson, would better serve the interest of working people?

B. Machinery of Empire

INTRODUCTION

From the realm of ideas we turn to consider how the Empire worked. Very hard, Kipling would say, as he draws attention to the unsung heroes of the Indian Civil Service (No. 20): so did Rhodes, driven by a colossal ambition (No. 21) and Milner, with lofty patriotism. (No. 22).

But the first Englishmen to penetrate a great many areas were missionaries. Their rôle in the process of empire-building is only now being fully evaluated, for here the historian has to detach himself not only from the Imperial past, but also from their religious outlook (No. 24); however, it is at once apparent from reading Livingstone (No. 23) and Paton (No. 26) that they regarded British rule as desirable, and strove to bring it about, because it would improve the quality of the lives of the natives concerned and increase the prospects of conversion.

The third section shows how the Empire functioned. Beginning with the Colonial Office in London, we see some of the deliberations concerned with establishing the British South Africa Company (No. 27). Next, we see another Chartered Company, the Royal Niger, extending the Empire by means of the blank treaty (No. 28). Indeed there were pressures to expand all the time, and the situation in Malaya is studied carefully by Governor Weld in a dispatch of the type that regularly came to London from all over the world (No. 29). However the Empire, if it were to have a future, had also to be won on the playing-fields of Eton and in the classrooms of Harrow, and school textbooks, among other things, saw to that (No. 30).

Yet difficulties constantly obstructed the Imperial drive. There were always people such as Frederic Harrison (No. 31) to question methods of government, while the great hope of the period for

some closer form of Imperial unity remained tantalizingly beyond
the bounds of practical politics (No. 33). The British Government,
having gained control of the great sea-lanes (No. 37), was more
interested in getting the colonies to share the burdens of defence
(Nos. 34 and 38).

By 1900, although more territory was British than ever before,
the settlement colonies were eager to work out their own destinies
(No. 39). Would the Empire disintegrate? Some, noting the
increasingly slippery grip Britain had on South African affairs,
felt the Empire might disintegrate if nothing were done for the
large colonial population oppressed by the Boers of the Transvaal.
Troop movements to South Africa provoked a Boer ultimatum,
and the Empire was at war.

Colonial contingents rushed to the fray, the sieges were raised
and there was much 'mafficking' much too soon. Before it was over,
there were 400,000 British troops in South Africa, the expression
'concentration camp' had been added to the language, and soon
war memorials spread across the land. In 1902, hostilities ceased
and Hobson's book appeared. In deed as in name, Imperialism
could never be the same again.

SECTION 4

PERSONNEL

20. *Rudyard Kipling (1865–1936) respected those who shouldered the
burden of Imperial rule, soldiers, road-builders, engineers, layers of
deep-sea cables. Such as these made Empire work. In a short story
'On the City Wall' published in his book* In Black and White *in
1889, Kipling paid tribute to the devoted English officials in India.*

. . . it is necessary to explain something about the Supreme
Government [of India] which is above all and below all and behind
all. Gentlemen come from England, spend a few weeks in India,
walk round this great Sphinx of the Plains, and write books upon
its ways and its works, denouncing or praising it as their own
ignorance prompts. Consequently all the world knows how the
Supreme Government conducts itself. But no one, not even the
Supreme Government, knows everything about the adminis-

tration of the Empire. Year by year England sends out fresh drafts for the first fighting line, which is officially called the Indian Civil Service. These die, or kill themselves by overwork, or are worried to death, or broken in health and hope in order that the land may be protected from death and sickness, famine and war, and may eventually become capable of standing alone. It will never stand alone, but the idea is a pretty one, and men are willing to die for it, and yearly the work of pushing and coaxing and scolding and petting the country into good living goes forward. If an advance be made all credit is given to the native, while the Englishmen stand back and wipe their foreheads. If a failure occurs the Englishmen step forward and take the blame.

21. *In this letter to the Under-Secretary for the Colonies, Sir Alfred (later Viscount) Milner (1854–1925), shrewdly assesses the strength and weaknesses of another great Empire builder in Southern Africa, Cecil Rhodes (1853–1902). Milner was British High Commissioner in South Africa between 1897 and 1905. Rhodes mixed high politics and big diamond and gold business with calculated daring. Both advanced British control in Africa and both played a leading part in precipitating the Boer War in 1899.*

There is a great deal you ought to know at home. I want to let you know as fast as I can find it out *with certainty* (I will not trouble you with mere guesses). But this kind of thing can only be communicated by letter. What I am in a hurry to write about today is *Rhodes*, especially with regard to the position in the North [Rhodesia]. ... It looks a small matter, but involves a large question, and with characteristic bigness of view he [Rhodes] at once so treated it. ... He looks to making the territory of the British South Africa Company [i.e. Rhodesia] into a separate Colony ultimately self-governed (the Company keeping its mineral and other valuable rights, but giving up administration). The Colony (which I may remark in passing, though nominally self-governed, will be virtually an absolute monarchy with Rhodes as monarch) he means to unite with Cape Colony and Natal [i.e. British South Africa], and then the three combined will bring *peaceful* pressure upon the [Boer] Republics to drive them into a S. African federation. For the execution of this big scheme he wants the new northern colony [Rhodesia] ... to be as big as possible. Therefore he wishes to incorporate the [Bechuanaland] Protectorate, and not to run the risk of something like a Crown Colony springing up between the Northern boundary of the Cape Colony and the territory already in the hands of the Company. In my opinion the policy, in the main, is good. Everything depends upon the execution. ... Rhodes is the only man big enough to carry out such a work, but on the other hand, Rhodes uncontrolled ... will probably fail in carrying it out, because he is too self-willed, too violent, too sanguine, and in too great a hurry. He is just the same man as he always was, undaunted and unbroken by his former failure [the Jameson Raid 1895], but also untaught by it. He is much too strong a man to be merely *used*. He will work for his own ends in his own way—we must accept that—but on the other hand we must, to a great extent, guide and restrain him. And unless he is to make shipwreck both of his own ambitions and our permanent interests, it is necessary that we should do so. The great question is, how, without unduly interfering with or worrying Rhodes, can we yet keep the necessary amount of control over him? ... We can keep a hold on him for the present *by means of the* [Bechuanaland] *Protectorate*. Here we have still, by the mercy of Providence, something which he dearly wishes to get hold of. ... If Rhodes wants it ... in order to get it he will behave himself as he never would, if there was not something which he wanted to get out of us. Men are ruled by their foibles, and Rhodes' foible is *size*. He really will be little or no better off for having the [Bechuanaland] Protectorate. It does not materially affect the game. But he looks at that big map. He sees on the one side the Cape Colony, of which he once was master and hopes to be again, on the other side Rhodesia, of which he is master. Between the two he sees that huge patch [the Bechuanaland Protectorate], which he all but got once and is still without. It makes his mouth water and he will do all he can to get it.

22. *Philip Kerr, later the Marquess of Lothian, (1882–1940) was one of the talented young men Milner gathered about him in South Africa after the Boer War. Kerr later promoted Imperial unity as editor of the magazine* Round Table. *This appreciation of Milner suggests the tension between the problem of reconciling the strong, and occasionally headstrong, authority of proconsuls like Milner with the need*

to follow British democratic practices. Milner was said to have been
prepared to face the suspension of the British constitution for the
sake of greater efficiency.

Lord Milner was a quite exceptional figure in English public
life. It is difficult to point to anybody quite like him. He was a
great proconsul and a great Civil Servant. But, unlike a Civil
Servant, he took the leading part in shaping the policy of his
country at a crisis in its history. Yet he had no real roots in the
political life of Great Britain. He never sat in the House of Commons. He was notoriously unpopular with the Conservative
Party machine. He was always a 'cross-bencher' in the House of
Lords.

Lord Milner was really a Roman of the Augustan age. Even his
appearance was strangely Caesarian. The absorbing passion of his
life was the British Empire. He worshipped it not because he was
fascinated by anything so futile as size, or because he liked to see
the map painted red, but because he had in his very bones that
great tradition of just and humane and efficient world-government
to which Rome gave birth and of which he saw in the British
Empire the greatest modern expression. Lord Milner slaved for
the Empire because he believed in the *Pax Britannica* as earlier
ages had longed for the *Pax Romana,* and because he saw in the
preservation and development of its administrative ideals the
principal hope for the progress of mankind.

The unsolved problem of Lord Milner's life was how to reconcile this great tradition of government with democracy. He was
not against popular government. His sympathy with the poor and
the oppressed, his contempt for the claims of wealth and privilege,
were too keen for him to believe in any system of class rule. But
he was unable to see how the democratic movement which was
sweeping everything before it in his time was to be made com-
patible with that scientific unity and order which he perceived to
be more than ever necessary in the complicated modern world.
In every fibre of his being he loathed the slipshod compromises,
the optimistic 'slogans', the vote-catching half-truths with which
democracy seemed to compromise the majestic governing art.

Here was the root of the quarrel between him and Liberalism.
He had none of that faith that the people often have vision to which
their rulers are blind, or that passionate conviction that it is better
for men to govern themselves badly and learn from their mistakes
than to be administered with supreme wisdom by somebody

R—C

else, which is, perhaps, the core of the Liberal creed. The only solution he could find was in race. Somehow wherever the British went their ideals of government went with them. And so he backed the British race. Some of his most criticized acts, and notably the Transvaal Chinese Labour Ordinance, were the outcome of the conviction that nothing save a sufficient leaven of British stock could ensure, not British rule, but British standards of government, overseas.

These opinions, coupled with great natural modesty and reserve, made him a very lonely figure. Everybody who worked with him came to admire him and to believe in him, even though they did not always agree with him. It was impossible not to love a character so faithful, so selfless, so sincere. But he himself fitted into no party and no group. The integrity and sensitiveness of his mind made it impossible for him to take his place in the normal party game, disqualified him indeed, for that rough-and-tumble of crude argument and cruder idealism and abuse which democracy still requires. When he did appear in public it was to speak his mind, exactly, honestly, without exaggeration or reserve, and to leave his hearers to take it or leave it as they chose . . . . History will remember Lord Milner chiefly for what he did in South Africa. . . . In Africa, to use an Americanism, he was the whole works. He determined the direction of British policy, he was the central figure in its execution, and he himself would wish his reputation to stand or fall by his work there.

To Liberals of an earlier age Sir Alfred Milner, as he then was, was the typical Jingo Imperialist. He was simply anathema to the Liberal mind. He certainly made some serious mistakes. But it is surely time that his fundamental work in South Africa should be viewed by Liberals in a truer perspective. Milner did not create the South African crisis. That crisis sprang from the fact that there were two powerful races in South Africa, the British and the Dutch, and that each had a focus in a government and a flag, in a country naturally meant to be one. Whatever chances there had been of a *modus vivendi* between the two were practically destroyed by the Jameson raid. From that moment it became inevitable that South Africa was going to be united under one or other of the two flags and of the two governmental ideals for which they stood.

Lord Milner early made up his mind that if he could help it South Africa was not going to be pushed, or cajoled, or coerced out of the Empire, and he put himself openly at the head of the party which stood for the British connection. President Kruger stood as inflexibly for the opposite solution. Neither side wanted war or plotted war. But both thought war a lesser evil than surrender, and they made their plans accordingly. The old dispute as to whether war could have been averted . . . will never be settled. For the real point is not whether war could have been avoided, but whether the crisis could have been solved in any any other way.

QUESTIONS:
1. List the reasons why Kipling is impelled to speak up for the I.C.S. official.
2. Consider the five documents on Milner and Rhodes (Nos. 6, 18, 21, 22, and 27). Both were working for the advancement of British interests in southern Africa: how different were their methods?

SECTION 5

MISSIONARIES

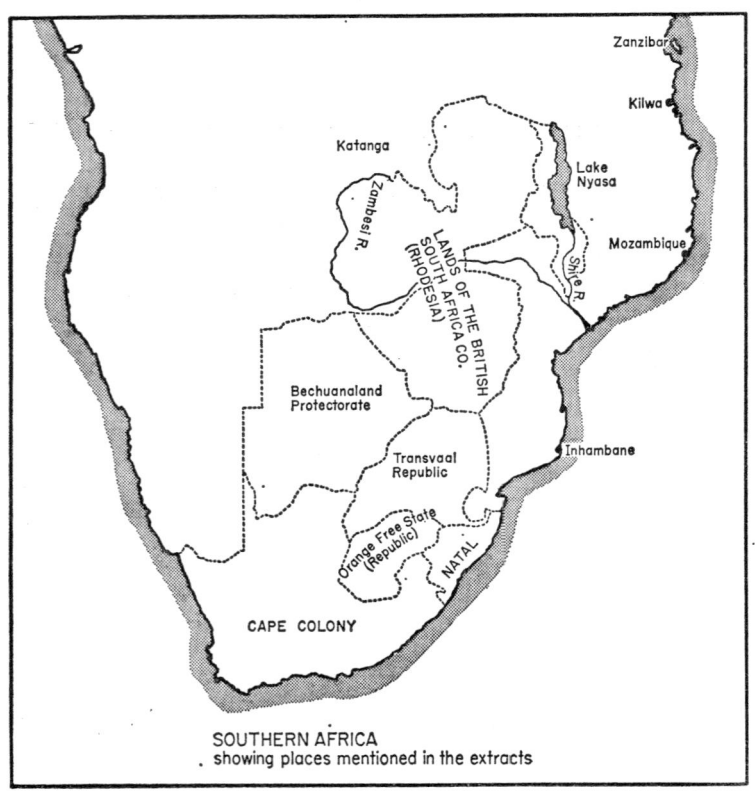

SOUTHERN AFRICA
. showing places mentioned in the extracts

23. *David Livingstone (1813–73) found that missionary work in Africa was checked by European ignorance of Central Africa. When he looked closer he found Central African society disrupted by the slave trade. Livingstone became, therefore, an explorer, writer and adviser about central African conditions. He hoped that missionaries would raise the individual African and that honest merchants would put slave traders out of business. As he worked and died working there, he inspired an unflagging British interest in Central Africa.*

The trade of Cazembé and Katanga's country, and of other parts of the interior, crosses Nyassa and the Shiré, on its way to the Arab port, Kilwa, and the Portuguese ports of Iboe and

Mozambique. At present, slaves, ivory, malachite, and copper ornaments, are the only articles of commerce. According to information collected by Colonel Rigby at Zanzibar, and from other sources, nearly all the slaves shipped from the above-mentioned ports were from the Nyassa district. By means of a small steamer, purchasing the ivory of the Lake and River above the cataracts, which together have a shoreline of at least 600 miles, the slave-trade in this quarter would be rendered unprofitable—for it is only by the ivory being carried by the slaves, that the latter do not eat up all the profits of a trip. An influence would be exerted over an enormous area of country, for the Mazitu about the north end of the Lake will not allow slave-traders to pass round that way through their country. They would be most efficient allies to the English, and might themselves be benefited by more intercourse. As things are now, the native traders in ivory and malachite have to submit to heavy exactions; and if we could give them the same prices which they at present get after carrying their merchandise 300 miles beyond this to the Coast, it might induce them to return without going further. It is only by cutting off the supplies in the interior, that we can crush the slave-trade on the Coast. The plan proposed would stop the slave-trade from the Zambesi on one side and Kilwa on the other; and would leave, beyond this tract, only the Portuguese port of Inhambane on the south, and a portion of the Sultan of Zanzibar's dominion on the north, for our cruisers to look after. The Lake people grow abundance of cotton for their own consumption, and can sell it for a penny a pound or even less. Water-carriage exists by the Shiré and Zambesi all the way to England, with the single exception of a portage of about thirty-five miles past the Murchison Cataracts, along which a road of less than forty miles could be made at a trifling expense; and it seems feasible that a legitimate and thriving trade might, in a short time, take the place of the present unlawful traffic. . . .

In this light, a European colony would be considered by the natives as an inestimable boon to inter-tropical Africa. Thousands of industrious natives would gladly settle round it, and engage in that peaceful pursuit of agriculture and trade of which they are so fond, and, undistracted by wars or rumours of wars, might listen to the purifying and ennobling truths of the gospel of Jesus Christ. The Manganja on the Zambesi, like their countrymen on the Shiré, are fond of agriculture; and, in addition to the usual varieties of food, cultivate tobacco and cotton in quantities more than equal to their wants. To the question, 'Would they work for

Europeans?' an affirmative answer may be given, if the Europeans belong to the class which can pay a reasonable price for labour, and not to that of adventurers who want employment for themselves.

24. *Bishop Tozer arrived in Central Africa in 1863 to find the mission on the shores of Lake Nyasa in a mess. Instead of Livingstone's scheme of a flourishing economy producing cotton, it produced martyrs, with few converts. Tozer therefore removed the mission at once to the coast for consolidation before again tackling the interior. Livingstone was most annoyed; but the bishop found enough work to do in Zanzibar. Here he describes the Muslim religion in a letter home:*

It is a kind of horrible parody of religion, pandering to every passion and lust, and utterly misrepresenting God and goodness. That Mahomet must have been a coarse, vulgar, treacherous man to invent a system which could lull his followers into security, and yet leave them as far from God as ever. This is our greatest hindrance. . . .

★25. Mary Kingsley (1862–1900) niece of the novelist Charles Kingsley, died of fever in South Africa during the Boer War. She pioneered scientific nature studies in West Africa, where she travelled widely. Her sharp eye and refusal to tolerate humbug made her a mature observer of the efforts of officials, traders, and missionaries.

The failure of the English Protestant missionaries in West Africa to recognize the differences between the minds of the Africans and their own, and their tendency to regard the African minds as so many jugs which have only to be emptied of the stuff which is in them and refilled with the particular doctrine they the missionaries are teaching, is certainly one of the primal causes of the mission failures, by eliminating those parts of the fetish that are a wholesome restraint and putting in their place the doctrine of forgiveness of sin by means of repentance. They intend to repent, it is true; but the popularity of a (to me) very unpleasant little hymn on the South-West Coast that has a chorus of

'A little talk with Jesus
Makes it right,
All right,'

demonstrates their view of the affair: no doubt sound doctrine but bad for Negro morals.

26. *In 1883 Australian authorities appealed to Britain for the annexation of the New Hebrides and other Pacific Islands which were thought to be the northern defence shield of Australia. The Rev. J. G. Paton (1824–1907), an outstanding Presbyterian missionary, pressed the Premier of the colony of Victoria to urge other Australian colonies to demand the annexation. There was an unusually happy coincidence of interests. As the Premier remarked, 'Politics, religion, commerce, civilization, humanity all pointed to the desirability of getting hold of these islands.' Paton put the case cogently, but nothing was done because Britain refused to move. Not till 1906 was a joint British and French government established in the New Hebrides.*

Sir,

For the following reasons we think the British Government ought now to take possession of the New Hebrides group of the South Sea Islands, of the Solomon group, and of all the intervening chain of islands from Fiji to New Guinea:

1. Because she has already taken possession of Fiji in the east, and we hope it will soon be known authoritatively that she has taken possession of New Guinea at the north-west adjoining her Australian possessions, and the islands between complete this chain of islands lying along the Australian coast. Taking possession of the New Hebrides would not add much to her expenses . . .

2. The sympathy of the New Hebrides natives are all with Great Britain, hence they long for British protection, while they fear and hate the French, who appear eager to annex the group, because they have seen the way the French have treated the native races in New Caledonia . . . and other South Seas Islands.

3. Till within the past few months almost all the Europeans on the New Hebrides were British subjects, who long for British protection.

4. All the men and all the money (over £140,000) used in civilizing and Christianizing the New Hebrides have been British. Now 14 missionaries and the Dayspring mission ship, and about 150 native evangelists and teachers are employed in the above work on this group, in which over £6,000 yearly of British and British-Colonial money is expended; and certainly it would be unwise to let any other power now take possession and reap the fruits of all this British outlay.

5. Because the New Hebrides are already a British dependency

in this sense—all its imports are from Sydney and Melbourne and British Colonies, and all its exports are also to British Colonies.

6. The islands of this group are generally very rich in soil and in tropical products so that if a possession of Great Britain, and the labour traffic stopped so as to retain what remains of the native populations on them, they would soon, and for ages to come, become rich sources of tropical wealth to these [Australasian] Colonies, as sugar cane is extensively cultivated on them by every native of the group, even in his heathen state. For natives they are an industrious, hard-working race. . . . The islands also grow maize, cotton, coffee, arrowroot, and spices, &c., and all tropical products could be largely produced on them.

7. Because if any other nation takes possession of them, their excellent harbours, as on Efate [New Hebridean central island], so well-supplied with the best fresh water, and their near proximity to Great Britain's Australasian Colonies, would in time of war make them dangerous to Britain's interests and commerce in the South Seas and to her Colonies.

8. The 13 islands of this group on which life and property are now comparatively safe, the 8,000 professed Christians on the group, and all the churches formed among them, are by God's blessing the fruits of the labours of British missionaries, who, at great toil, expense, and loss of life, have translated, got printed, and taught the natives to read the Bible in part or in whole in nine different languages of this group, while 70,000 at least are longing and ready for the gospel. On this group 21 members of the mission families died or were murdered by the savages in beginning God's work among them, not including good Bishop Paterson, of the Melanesian Mission, and we fear all this good work would be lost if the New Hebrides fall into other than British hands.

9. Because we see no other way of suppressing the labour traffic in Polynesia, with all its many evils, as it rapidly depopulates the islands, being attended by much bloodshed, misery, and loss of life. It is an unmitigated evil to the natives, and ruinous to all engaged in it, and to the work of civilizing and Christianizing the islanders, while all experience proves that all labour laws and regulations, with Government agents and gunboats, cannot prevent such evils, which have always been the sad accompaniments of all such traffic in men and women in every

land, and because this traffic and its evils are a sad stain on our British glory and Australasian honour, seeing Britain has done so much to free the slave and suppress slavery in other lands.

For the above reasons, and others that might be given we sincerely hope and pray that you will do all possible to get Victoria and the other Colonial Governments to help and unite in urging Great Britain at once to take possession of the New Hebrides group. Whether looked at in the interests of humanity, or of Christianity, or commercially, or politically, surely it is most desirable that they should be at once British possessions; hence we plead for your judicious and able help, and remain, your humble servant,

JOHN G. PATON
Senior Missionary,
New Hebrides Mission.

QUESTIONS:
1. How did Livingstone hope to stamp out the slave trade in Central Africa?
2. What changes in Central African society, according to Livingstone, would give missionaries a greater chance of success?
3. How would some missionary methods and attitudes seem to have handicapped British missionary work in Africa?
4. Consider Paton's arguments for British annexation of the New Hebrides:
   (a) What do Paton's arguments suggest were the main incentives for extension of empire in the Pacific?
   (b) Do you think Paton put up a case strong enough to justify annexation?
   (c) Was Paton, as a missionary in his time and place, inevitably an agent for the extension of the British Empire?

SECTION 6

PROCESSES

27. *This Colonial Office letter shows the dilemma of the British Government's imperial policy in Africa. The Foreign Office under Lord Salisbury wanted no international incidents, the Colonial Office*

under Lord Knutsford wanted no heavy financial commitments
arising from reckless extension of British influence in tropical Africa.
A powerful but properly controlled Chartered Company would
extend British influence, save money and political embarrassment.

Colonial Office to Foreign Office

Downing Street, May 16th, 1889.

Sir,

I am directed by Lord Knutsford to transmit to you the en-
closed copies of correspondence between this Department and
Lord Gifford, v.c., Chairman of the Exploring Company (Limited)
relative to the grant of a Royal Charter to a company to be formed
for developing the Bechuanaland Protectorate and the countries to
the north.

I am also to enclose a copy of a letter from Mr. C. J. Rhodes,
of the Cape Colony, and two other gentlemen, who, as represent-
ing the holders of what is called the Rudd Concession from Lo
Bengula, state that they have arranged with Lord Gifford's
Company to co-operate in any such scheme as that proposed.
In fact, it is understood that the combination, of which Lord
Gifford and Mr. Rhodes are the leaders, hope to be able to unite
most if not all the existing British interests in the Protectorate
and the countries to the northwards.

I am to observe that, in consenting to consider this scheme in
more detail, Lord Knutsford has been influenced by the consideration that if such a company is incorporated by Royal Charter
its constitution, objects, and operations will become more directly
subject to control by Her Majesty's Government than if it were
left to these gentlemen to incorporate themselves under the Joint
Stock Companies Acts, as they are entitled to do. In the latter
case, Her Majesty's Government would not be able effectually to
prevent the company from taking its own line of policy, which
might possibly result in complications with Native Chiefs and
others, necessitating military expenditure and perhaps even
military operations. The example of the Imperial East African
Company shows that such a body may to some considerable
extent relieve Her Majesty's Government from diplomatic
difficulties and heavy expenditure. In Lord Knutsford's judgment
such a company as that proposed for the Bechuanaland Protectorate, if well conducted, would render still more valuable assistance
to Her Majesty's Government in South Africa.

At present nothing could be more unsatisfactory than the

condition of things existing in that quarter. Every year large
grants have to be obtained from Parliament nominally in aid of
civil expenditure, but almost altogether swallowed up in the
maintenance of a semi-military police force, whilst the peace of
the country is by no means as well assured as it ought to be, and
fresh demands are being made on Her Majesty's Government for
further expenditure on an increase of the police and telegraph
construction, pronounced to be absolutely necessary for the safety
of the country.

Lord Knutsford would suggest, for Lord Salisbury's consideration, whether, if a charter is granted, the company might not
with advantage be required to include within its sphere, in the first
instance or at some later period, such portion of territory north
of the Zambesi as it may be important to control with a view to the
security of communications with the Shiré and Lake Nyassa, and
the protection of British missionary settlements. I am, &c.,
[To] *The Under-Secretary of State,*   (*Signed*) JOHN BRAMSTON.
Foreign Office.

28. *Between 1884 and 1892 over 350 Nigerian chiefs made treaties
with the Royal Niger Company, which advanced British commercial
activities in what is now Nigeria. Blank treaty forms were carried
by Company agents. Different circumstances required distinct forms.
This treaty form was used some 13 times in 1889 and 1890.*

FORM NO. 9

TREATY made on the   day of   , 18 , between
the Chiefs of   on the one hand, and the Royal
Niger Company (Chartered and Limited), hereinafter called
'the Company' on the other hand.

1. We, the Undersigned Chiefs of   , with the
consent of our people, and with the view of bettering their
condition, do this day cede to the Company, and their
assigns, for ever, the whole of our territory; but the Company
shall pay private owners a reasonable amount for any portion
of land that the Company may require from time to time.

2. We hereby give to the Company and their assigns, for ever,
full jurisdiction of every kind; and we pledge ourselves not
to enter into any war with other tribes without the sanction
of the Company.

3. We also give to the Company and their assigns, for ever, the sole right to mine in our territory.

4. In consideration of the foregoing, the Company bind themselves not to interfere with any of the native laws or customs of the country, except so far as may be necessary for good government and the maintenance of order.

5. The Company bind themselves to protect, as far as practicable, the said Chiefs from the attacks of any neighbouring aggressive tribes.

6. In consideration of the above, the Company have this day paid the said Chiefs of   goods to the value of   , receipt of which is hereby acknowledged.

This Agreement having been interpreted to us, the abovementioned Chiefs of   , we hereby approve, and accept it for ourselves and for our people with their consent, and, in testimony of this, having no knowledge of writing, do affix our marks below it, and I,   , for and on behalf of the Company, do hereby affix my hand.

We, the Undersigned witnesses, do hereby solemnly declare that the Chiefs whose names are placed opposite their respective marks have in our presence affixed their marks of their own free will and consent, and the said   has, in our presence, affixed his signature.

For the Royal Niger Company (Chartered and Limited)

Declaration by Interpreter

I,   , native of   do hereby solemnly declare that I am well acquainted with the   language, and that on the   day of   18   , I truly and faithfully explained the above Agreement to all the native signatories whose marks are affixed to this Treaty, and that they understood its meaning.

Witnesses to the above   mark signature: Done in triplicate at   this   day of 18   .

---

29. *Sir Frederick Weld (1823–91) had been Premier of New Zealand and Governor of Western Australia and Tasmania successively, when he was appointed Governor of the Straits Settlements in 1880. Arriving back in Singapore after a tour of the Malay States, he*

aired his thoughts on a great many matters in a dispatch to the Colonial Secretary, Lord Kimberley.
(*a*) *One problem was to have a clear statement of British Policy.*

It seems self evident that interests affecting not only the welfare and position of large bodies of men who look to us for aid, but of a country which is the key to the Far East, should not be left to chance dealing—and I may presume that the Home Government has considered or is considering its future policy in regard to the Malay States of the Peninsula; nevertheless no indication of that policy has so far as I am aware even confidentially reached my predecessors; yet a Governor acting, as he sometimes must act, on sudden occasion or emergency will if he has any statesmanlike ability be guided in his action by his idea of what either must or of what ought to be the policy of the future, and consequently it seems to me that your Lordship cannot be kept too exactly informed of the views held by the representatives of the Crown in this colony. . . .

(*b*) *He then proceeds to discuss the extreme delicacy of relations with the Native States, which were not under direct rule but retained their own governments under British protection and supervision.*

The Native States are now unquestionably in a satisfactory position and every year of peace, prosperity and progress renders it less likely that the present state of affairs will be disturbed, but nevertheless some years must elapse before good government can be said to be secured on a firm basis—any moment some slight matter, the indiscretion not only of a Resident but of a subordinate, might lead to difficulties, and it is impossible with the men and means at our command, or indeed with any given men and means, to be sure that no such accident may occur. . . .
The present theory of the Native States Government is simply that we advise and we do not assume the possibility of our advice not being taken—Notwithstanding this, just before my arrival, the Administrator acting under instruction from England declined to permit the Resident of Sungei Ujong to give any advice whatever in regard to the election of the new Datu Klana [ruler]. I am myself of opinion that it was wise for some reasons to leave that election quite free though some very guarded indication of the views of Government might be often given with advantage

in such cases, and in other possible ones more decided action might be absolutely necessary.

But immediately afterwards the question arose, if the Resident will not advise upon the election of the new Datu Klana and has no hand in his making, on what ground can he presume to advise the levy of taxes, decline to recommend pensions we want, and prevent us, the chiefs of Sungei Ujong, from exacting imposts from the people for our own purposes—The only answer is: because in the one case it was not seen fit that he should interfere and in the other it is held to be advisable. It is for the Government to judge what is best.

As a matter of fact our advice in financial matters, in criminal cases, and in the prevention of oppression of the weak—of slaves and slavegirls, is often merely taken because it is supposed that what we 'advise', we mean must be done, and that we are considered powerful enough to insist upon it, as the Police forces in the protected States are entirely under the control of the Resident. It stands to reason that a Rajah who has hitherto been subject to no law but his own pleasure does not like to be forced to set free a girl whom he forcibly detains and ill-treats, or to deliver up to justice his relative who has stabbed a 'mere' Chinaman—or to be prevented from making requisitions at will on his weak neighbours when he is impecunious. . . .

Looking most hopefully as I do on the excellent work we are doing on the Peninsula and never doubting its success, it is still impossible to shut my eyes to the fact that we are and have been relying on something more than simple advice and must continue however unostentatiously to do so unless we are preparing to retire from the country. . . .

(c) *In the last part of the dispatch Sir Frederick considers the future of the region. He concludes that whether the existing state of affairs is allowed to continue or not, British withdrawal is unthinkable.*

I concur with Sir William Robinson in thinking that did we so abandon them their state would probably be worse than it was when we first intervened. I do not think that anything could justify us in leaving them to anarchy, and our own interests as well as theirs forbid it—Nothing that we have done has taught them to govern themselves, we are merely teaching them to co-operate with us in governing under our guidance. I have always held the theory that to teach men to govern themselves you must throw them a good deal on their own resources; we are doing, necessarily doing, the very reverse. Moreover I doubt if Asiatics will ever learn to govern themselves [added in margin: I mean in the sense of popular government], it is contrary to the genius of their race, of their history, of their religious systems that they should— Their desire is a mild just and firm despotism; that we can give them.

30. *Textbook writers change little. We express the views of our generation as briefly, clearly, and as confidently as possible. A master at Harrow School and a former Cambridge Fellow here tried his hand about 1901 in* A Brief Survey of British History.

Britain has contented herself in the past with the few treaty ports which China has unwillingly opened. But she cannot see China closed to her, as it would be were it to pass into Russian hands, or even were it partitioned up. And both France and Germany have cast covetous eyes on it, so that a 'scramble for China' may perhaps follow the 'scramble for Africa'. Thus we have declared for the policy of the 'open door', which means that we will not suffer China to be closed to our trade. We have answered the German seizure of Kiao-chau and the Russian seizure of Port Arthur by demanding Wei-Hai-Wei as a naval station. But the difficulties of resisting Russia in China are very great. In the far East the Russian is himself half an Oriental, with all the Eastern's capacity for promising what he does not mean to perform; yet he cannot be dealt with as Britain has often dealt with treacherous Eastern rulers, namely, by a bombardment which brings them to their senses, because the Russian has the weight of a great European power behind him. Thus the course of events in China is bound to give us many an anxious hour in the future.

*31. *Governor Weld, in his opening remarks, spoke of the difficulties that arise when a governor has to act promptly in an emergency. This was precisely the situation that faced Governor Eyre in Jamaica in 1865, when a Negro rising broke out in the east of the island. He acted promptly, perhaps savagely; and in the belief that his leading opponent in the Assembly had incited the rising, had him removed to the military district, court-martialled and hanged. The news of those events caused a great stir in England, and Governor Eyre returned to find himself charged with murder. He was acquitted, but the case served to check arbitrary justice in the tropical colonies.*

Frederic Harrison (1831–1923) was a member of the Committee set up to bring Eyre to justice. He set forth his views in a series of letters sent to the Daily News *in November and December, 1866.*

Sir,—I have hitherto attempted to show that in the recent events in Jamaica gross breaches of law were committed by the Government. I will now try to point out how essential it is to this nation that these breaches of law should not pass without condemnation. . . .

I have said hitherto nothing about the Negroes. But it is not that they are forgotten: the oft-recurring tale is too frightfully reiterated ever to pass from the memory of humanity. It is a tale of wonderful sameness—one unbroken weary round of horror. A riot; much agitation; a good deal of plunder; a little bloodshed; then an ominous pause. Soon an organized reign of terror by the planters, martial law, burnings, floggings, torturings, and indiscriminate massacre of an unresisting and cowering people, protracted for months, until the very executioners become exhausted. Afterward a murmur of indignation at home, defiance from the planter interest, a craven government, and public apathy. Such is the British rule in the West Indies. . . . Turn to the effect of this case upon our whole colonial Empire. That empire is very vast and very composite. There is but one law for it. In principle, in the eye of justice, every citizen within it has equal rights. Civilly we have no classes of citizenship. Every citizen in that empire, black or white, is perilled by the sanction of outrage on any other. We cannot make rules for Negroes without baiting them like traps for Europeans . . . English law is of that kind, that, if you play fast and loose with it, it vanishes. . . . What is done in a colony today may be done in Ireland tomorrow, and in England hereafter. . . .

QUESTIONS:
1. What do you learn about the Royal Niger Company from the blank treaty? What rights does it guarantee the Africans?
2. In what ways did a British Resident in a Malay State make his presence felt? What, in Governor Weld's view, was the major difficulty?
3. What were the reasons, as Weld saw them, justifying British control of Malaya?
4. In what ways are both the Chartered Company and the Native Protected State varieties of indirect rule?
5. Why was Harrison anxious to bring Governor Eyre to justice?

SECTION 7

TOWARDS IMPERIAL UNITY

32. *George Parkin (1846–1922), a Canadian-born enthusiast for British Imperial causes, was one of the most active and eloquent public speakers in favour of a united government of all the white English-speaking members of the British Empire. In England his personal force and zeal converted many, including Milner. His arguments caught many passing attitudes and fancies. He was a respected Imperial lecturer in a golden age of preaching by convinced believers.*

It may be fairly claimed that in accepting the federal idea Anglo-Saxon peoples have reached the crown of their political achievement, inasmuch as it offers a compromise between ex-cessively centralized systems of government, which gave strength at the expense of local freedom, and those other systems which for the sake of local freedom sacrificed the strength which was necessary for their own preservation.

... Federalism is the device by which organized democracy, without giving up anything essential to liberty, is placed in a position to wrestle on even terms with organized despotism.

... But objections to federal organization for the Empire are at once raised. 'The areas and communities to be dealt with are too vast, the problem too complex and the consequent difficulty of getting an adequate organization too great for such a plan to be thought of.' To this it may be answered that the growth of the United States has widened political horizons.

... But in the United States, in Canada, in Australia it is urged, we have continental contiguity. The British Empire is too large, its parts separated by oceans, are unfitted for govern-ment under a common federal system. We can at least answer that the standard of possible size for a nation has steadily enlarged in the course of history. ...

For great trading communities, moreover, we must remember that oceans do not divide. The almost instantaneous transmission of thought, the cheap transmission of goods, the speedy travel possible for men have revolutionized pre-existing conditions in commerce and society, once more widening our horizon.

... No limit can be put to the range of common interest between communities of which one devotes its industry chiefly to supplying the raw material of commerce, the other [i.e. Britain] to its manufacture.

This community of industrial influence is strengthened by a thousand influences. . . .

The population which flows into the waste places of the colonies comes chiefly from the motherland, not driven out by religious persecution or political tyranny, but impelled by the spirit of enterprise or in search of the larger breathing and working space of new countries. In almost every case the emigrant makes a new bond of friendly connection. . . .

Admitting the difficulties involved in framing a Federal system we must at the same time remember the long and peculiar training which our race has had in dealing with them. . . . The experience of the United States. . . . Canada faced the question a quarter of a century ago. . . . Encouraged by these examples, Australia is taking steps to frame a similar union. . . .

A colony now has no power of making peace or war; no voice, save by courtesy of the mother-country, in making treaties; no direct influence on the exercise of national diplomacy. Admitted to an organic union, its voice would be heard and its influence felt in the decision of those questions. . . . With enlarged powers, it is true, the colony would have to accept enlarged responsibilities. . . .

Surely this is not subtracting anything from the power of self-government. It is the means of making it complete. Shall it then be separation or close union?

*33. *E. A. Freeman (1823–92) a fluent writer and able controversialist, made rash public statements all his life. Sometimes he won. Sometimes he lost. He became Regius Professor of Modern History at Oxford at the age of sixty-one and continued to dispute. This extract shows his power: he is using imperialist rhetoric to demolish the imperialist argument.*

As yet, the doctrine of Imperial Federation is somewhat vague, and its objects are somewhat fluctuating. Sometimes we are told that the Imperial Federation is to be a union of all English-speaking people. The wiser advocates of the scheme see the difficulties, but they seem for the nonce to put them in their pockets. They do not talk either of a federation of all English-speaking people or of a federation of all the Queen's dominions.

They mention those parts of the Queen's dominions, those parts of the English-speaking people, to which they wish their scheme of federation to extend, and they say nothing about any other parts of either. But this is not to go to the root of the matter, and it is humdrum work compared with the talk of the more enthusiastic votaries of 'Imperial Federation'. It is to be the 'federation of the Empire', that is presumably of the whole 'Empire', and in some of the highest flights it would sometimes seem as if the 'federation of the Empire', and the 'federation of all English-speaking people' were the same thing. . . .

If we are to have a real federation of the Empire, the whole people of the Empire must be let in with full federal rights, as political equals of the Englishman of Britain and the Englishman of Australia. But this would be something very different from a federation of the English-speaking people. Such an enfranchisement as this would indeed be a leap in the dark, a leap such as no people ever took before. It is not for us to say what would be likely to come of it; let us rather ask those who talk about Imperial Federation whether they have thought what would be likely to come of it. Whenever the thing is to talk big about 'empire', its greatness, its 'prestige', all about the dominion on which the sun never sets, all about the drum-roll of the British Army going the round of the world, then India is the dearest, the most cherished, the sublimest, part of the talk. 'Imperial' interests, 'imperial' greatness, 'imperial' everything, seem specially at home in that land. It is the specially imperial soil. 'Our Eastern Empire,' 'our Indian Empire,' is the grandest subject of all for magnificent eloquence. And why? To speak the plain truth, because here the corporate Emperor 'We' comes in on the grandest scale. 'We' govern India; 'we' hold the dominion of Aurungzebe [Mughal Emperor]; is not every British elector part of a great corporate Aurungzebe? But receive India to federation, and 'we' cease to do all this. In a federation of the 'Empire', 'we' must simply sink into the position of citizens of one or more of its states; the elector for London will be in no way privileged above the elector for Masulipatam. It may even be that the 'we' shall be turned about, and that people at Masulipatam will begin to say how 'we' govern England. Instead of every British elector being part of a corporate Aurungzebe, it may be that every Indian elector shall be part of a corporate William [the Conqueror]. Imperial Federation may take a shape in which England, Scotland, Canada, Australia, shall be dependencies of the Empire of India. For truly it will need some

very artificial arrangement to secure even proportional represent-
ation for any of those small and distant cantons, lying so far away
from the main centre of power and population.

34. *In 1887, Queen Victoria had reigned for fifty years. The British
at home and in the colonies were jubilant: and in London the occasion
was marked by the first Colonial Conference. However the Prime
Minister, the Marquess of Salisbury (1830–1903) spoke very guard-
edly about Imperial Federation to the Premiers assembled.*

The business that brings you here today is of a peculiar character, due to the very peculiar character of the Empire over which the
Queen rules. It yields to none—it is, perhaps, superior to all—in
its greatness, in its extent, in the vastness of its population, and the
magnificence of its wealth. But it has this peculiarity which dis-
tinguishes it from other Empires—a want of continuity; it is
separated into parts by stretches of ocean; and what we are here
today for is to see how far we must acquiesce in the conditions
which that separation causes, how far we can obliterate them by
agreement and by organization. I am not here now to recommend
you to indulge in any ambitious schemes of constitution making.
I saw in the papers (I do not know if it was true) that some of the
most important Colonies have telegraphed to their representatives
not to take part in any scheme of Imperial Federation. If that is
so, I think those Colonies are only wise. That is a matter for the
future rather than for the present. . . .

We cannot emulate the German Empire in conducting all our
Imperial affairs from one centre; whether we shall ever be able to
do so I do not know; but for the present we must reconcile
ourselves to conducting our own affairs, so far as domestic matters
go, each in its own locality; and so far as our experience of that
practice has gone it has succeeded fairly well. But there are other
matters that are not quite so distant. Before the German Empire
came to its present condition it had two forms of Union, both of
which I think might be possible in an Empire such as ours, though
both, perhaps, are not possible now. There was the Zollverein,
the Customs Union and there was the Kriegsverein, the Union
for military purposes. I fear that we must for the present put in
the distant and shadowy portion of our task, and not in the practical part of it, any hope of establishing a Custom Union among the
various parts of the Empire. I do not think that in the nature of

things it is impossible; I do not think that the mere fact that we are separated by the sea renders it impossible. But the resolutions which were come to in respect to our fiscal policy forty years ago set any such possibility entirely aside, and it cannot be now resumed until on one side or the other very different notions with regard to fiscal policy prevail from those which prevail at the present moment. I will pass that by, and merely point your attention to the Kriegsverein, which I believe is the real and most important business upon which you will be engaged; that is to say, the Union for purposes of mutual defence. That is the business which the Conference has now before it.

35. *From the speech of Joseph Chamberlain (1836–1914), Secretary of State for the Colonies 1895–1903, who introduced the Bill for the establishment of the Federal Commonwealth of Australia in the House of Commons, May 14th 1900. Chamberlain upheld the superior authority of the British Parliament over any colonial authority.*

This Bill, which is the result of careful and prolonged labours of the ablest statesmen in Australia, enables that great island continent to enter at once the widening circle of English-speaking nations. No longer will she be a congeries of States, each of them separate from and entirely independent of the others, a position which any one will see might possibly in the future, through the natural consequences of competition, become a source of danger or lead, at any rate, to friction and to weakness. But, if this Bill passes, in future Australia will be, in the words of the preamble of the Bill which I am about to introduce, 'an indissoluble federal Commonwealth firmly united for many of the most important functions of government'. . . . We believe that it is in the interest of Australia, and that has always been with us the first consideration. But we recognize that it is also in our interest as well; we believe the relations between ourselves and these colonies will be simplified, will be more frequent and unrestricted . . . when we have to deal with a single central authority instead of having severally to consult six independent Governments. . . . The Bill has been prepared without reference to us . . . and although I am convinced that the Australian people will be neither offended nor insulted if we alter here a word or there a word, or even a clause in this Bill, I think, on the other hand they do expect that we shall have a reasonable regard to the labours . . . and to the general feeling of the Australian people, wherever it has been really and conclusively shown, and to those rights of self government of which they have made so magnificent a use and which we have so freely and gladly conceded. . . . [We] have accepted without demur, and we shall ask the House of Commons to accept, every point in this Bill, every word, every line, every clause, which deals exclusively with the interests of Australia. We may be vain enough to think that we might have made improvements for the advantage of Australia, but we recognize that they are the best judges in their own case. . . . But . . . wherever the Bill touches the interests of the Empire as a whole, or the interests of Her Majesty's subjects, or of Her Majesty's possessions outside Australia, the Imperial Parliament occupies a position of trust which it is not the desire of the Empire, and which I do not believe for a moment it is the desire of Australia, that we should fulfil in any perfunctory or formal manner. . . .

[Some amendments were indeed made by the Imperial Parliament in the name of Imperial Unity. Appeal from Australia to the Judicial Committee of the Privy Council was made easier and Australian Federal legislation was not allowed to conflict with Imperial legislation.]

36. *The highest law court of the British Empire, the Judicial Committee of the Privy Council was, and is, a venerable company of elder judges specially selected. This Committee was the logical climax of the rule of law which was frequently on the lips of supporters of the British Empire. In 1900, Stanley Leighton, M.P., (1837–1901) commented to the House of Commons that the Committee although impressive, remained obscure.*

. . . very few people knew what the Judicial Committee of the Privy Council was, of whom it was composed, what it did, and where it held court. He [Stanley Leighton] had determined ten years ago to make a search and make quite sure that it had not only a name but a local habitation, and he inquired of all his friends 'Where is the Privy Council?' and no one knew. He asked judges and the like and was referred to 'Whitaker' and a little book entitled, 'Things Not Generally Known', from neither of which could he extract the desired information. He then conceived the idea of starting at the top of Parliament Street and knocking at every door and inquiring if the Privy Council was at home, and in the course of his peregrinations he came to a door at which a policeman was standing, who, in answer to his inquiries, directed him up a small back staircase, and upon entering a small room on the second floor he found himself in the presence of the august assembly. There was no accommodation for strangers. It was not surprising that in such a position of obscurity this august Council was hardly appreciated or even known.

QUESTIONS:
1. Why was Imperial Federation suggested?
2. Salisbury was unwilling to consider Imperial Federation. Why? What forms of association did he prefer?
3. From a reading of Freeman and Parkin what would you say were the difficulties confronting any scheme of Imperial Federation?
4. What does the Chamberlain document tell us about Britain's relations with the self-governing colonies by 1900?

SECTION 8

IMPERIAL DEFENCE

37. *Benjamin Disraeli, the Prime Minister, explained to the House of Commons on February 21st, 1876, the purchase by the British Government of shares worth £4,000,000 in the Suez Canal Company. They were bought from the ruler of Egypt, financially desperate.*

What we have to do tonight is to agree to the Vote for the purchase of these shares. I have never recommended, and I do not now recommend this purchase as a financial investment. If it gave us 10 per cent of interest and a security as good as the Consols, I do not think an English minister would be justified in making such an investment; still less if he is obliged to borrow the money for the occasion. I do not recommend it either as a commercial speculation, although I believe that many of those who have looked upon it with little favour will probably be surprised with the pecuniary results of the purchase. I have always, and do now recommend it to the country as a political transaction, and one which I believe is calculated to strengthen the Empire. That is the spirit in which it has been accepted by the country. ... They want the Empire to be maintained, to be strengthened; they will not be alarmed even if it be increased. Because they think we are obtaining a great hold and interest in this important portion of Africa—because they believe that it secures a highway to our Indian Empire and our other dependencies, the people of England have from the first recognized the propriety and the wisdom of the step which we shall sanction tonight.

38. *The British Empire depended for its prosperity and economic survival on its sea-borne trade which was protected by the British Navy.*
 An Admiralty statement (here selectively adapted) about Empire trade and naval maintenance costs was submitted to the meeting of the British Government with the self-governing colonial government leaders at the Colonial Conference of 1902 and amended in 1903.

(*a*) The annual value of British Empire trade in 1900

	£
Trade of United Kingdom with Foreign Countries	711,838,000
Trade of United Kingdom with British Dominions beyond the Seas	237,098,000
Total ..	£948,936,000
Trade of British Dominions beyond the Seas with Foreign Countries and among themselves ..	254,342,000
Total Trade of Empire ..	£1,203,278,000

... It will be seen that about one-fifth of the Total Trade of the Empire is not directly connected with the United Kingdom.

(*b*) The annual cost of maintaining British Naval Squadrons in all seas. The original cost of building the ships is not included.

I. *The Atlantic Ocean*

	£
North America and West Indian	330,000
Cape of Good Hope	396,000
South-East Coast of America	76,000
	£802,000

II. Eastern Seas and Pacific

		£
China [station]	.. ..	1,430,000
East Indies ..	.. ..	303,000
Australia ..	.. ..	312,000
	Total Eastern Seas ..	£2,045,000
	Pacific	202,000
	Total.. ..	£2,247,000

(*c*) Of this Naval maintenance cost of £2,247,000 in 1900 the self-governing colonies contributed:

		£
Australia	.. ..	75,500
British South Africa	.. .. ..	42,000
New Zealand	.. ..	15,500
Canada	.. ..	nil
	Total	£133,000

Canada was prevented from contributing by a strong French–Canadian opposition to helping British imperial strength.

(*d*) The Admiralty statement also went beyond mere maintenance costs for Naval Squadrons.

For 1902 the Navy Estimates accounted for £31,255,500 which was equal to a contribution of 15*s*. 1*d*. per head of the population of the United Kingdom. If this had been divided equally per head among the white population of the Empire, the charge per head would have amounted to 12*s*. 0¼*d*. An appendix showed that naval expenditure per head of population in the self-governing colonies amounted to:

British South Africa:

		s.	*d.*
Natal	.. .. .. ••	4	5¾
Cape of Good Hope	.. ..	1	1¼
Australia	.. ..	0	10¾
New Zealand	.. ..	0	6½
Canada	.. ••		nil

*39. *The rise of British Imperialism occasioned sporadic outbursts of colonial nationalism, equally vehement and keenly argued. The* Sydney Bulletin *regularly commented on what seemed to add to or detract from a distinctively Australian view of life. By 1903 the idea of paying additional Australian tribute money to London for naval defence goaded the* Bulletin *into characteristic indignation.*

THE NAVAL AGREEMENT OF 1902

From whatever point of view—imperial or anti-imperial—the scheme is considered, its only logical defence lies in the theory that Australia is a poor, forsaken country, without administrative brains, courage, enterprise, or intelligence, not fit to have any dignified part in its own naval defence, not to be trusted with any weapons lest it should misuse them, worth only to drudge for the money which a higher and more capable power shall spend and to provide the lob-lolly boys, the slushes and the deck-swabbers, whose efforts a higher power shall direct and control. . . . The alternative to the naval tribute, proposed by Mr. Barton, is the expenditure of a like sum of money, or, if necessary, a much larger sum of money, on an Australian Navy, which would be organized on the same lines as the Australian Army, and would probably be, for some time at least, commanded by a British admiral, and to a very considerable extent officered by Britishers. This navy would, in times of peace, be used as a training squadron for Australian naval men. In times of war it would be available for the defence of Australia and, there is no doubt, for the assistance of Britain in other waters, if that were called for. The service to the Empire in merely maintaining the coaling and victualling stations in these waters, in providing and keeping up a base for the British forces, would be immense. . . . Further, by setting up a standard of independent, though sympathetic organization it would give a standard of comparison and of emulation now wanting. In the South African War, Australian soldiers were able to give valuable points to British Tommies in cow-stealing, farm-burning, and concentrating, as well as in other and more dignified branches of the art of war. It is reasonable to suppose that an Australian Navy would, like an Australian Army, develop points in tactics and in management which would be of value to the Britisher. The Lords of the Admiralty are supposed now to be perfect—as the War Office was supposed to be perfect five years ago. But it is possible to imagine that there are faults in the Navy, as there were in the Army; that a fine tradition has been allowed to congeal into a dead and apathetic routine, and that a naval war would show as alarming faults in Britain's sea-power as the last campaign showed in its land forces. The payment by Australia of £240,000 a year would do nothing to correct these faults, if they do exist, but the gradual evolution of an Australian fleet, based on the British model but not bound by sacrosanct tradition to follow that model in every detail, would provide an invaluable standard of comparison and of criticism. The free and easy Australian soldier [has had his reforming services to the British Army very freely acknowledged. . . . It is more than possible that with the growth of an Australian Navy a future generation of British might be expressing equally devout thanks for free-and-easy Australian naval men.

QUESTIONS:
1. What did Disraeli mean when he called the acquisition of the Suez Canal shares 'a political transaction'?
2. Imperial defence seems to have been mainly Imperial naval defence. Why was Imperial army defence less important?
3. Suggest some of the difficulties in arranging a fair distribution of the payment and burden of Imperial naval defence.

GENERAL QUESTIONS:

1. Why did Britain regard India as an important part of her Empire?
2. What was Jingoism? How did Jingoism make imperial expansion easier to undertake and accept?
3. What do you understand by a belief in British national destiny in this period?
4. How much awareness of British economic interests do you find in Imperialism?
   Were these interests assisted by belief in British national destiny?
5. Frederic Harrison (No. 31) asserted that all Empire citizens should enjoy equal rights. Can you suggest any difficulties in the way of such equality?
6. Some Empire builders like Milner and Rhodes seemed to prefer the use of absolute authority rather than democratic methods in the rule of the Empire. Was this a common tendency as far as you can see? Do you think that there was any danger that British home politics might be threatened by absolute methods used in parts of the Empire?

Sources of Extracts

1   Anthony Trollope, *The West Indies* (Chapman and Hall, 1859), pp. 83, 84, 85

2   Anthony Trollope, ed. B. A. Booth, *The Tireless Traveller* (University of California Press, 1941), pp. 199–200

3   C. W. Dilke, *Greater Britain* (John Murray, 1868), Vol. I, pp. vii–viii; Vol. II, p. 405

4   *Fortnightly Review*, 1870, p. 705

5   J. A. Froude, *Oceana*, 1886 (quoted Longman's Silver Library ed., 1898, pp. 104, 105, 106)

6   *The Times*, July 27th, 1925

7   J. Bonwick, *The Lost Tasmanian Race* (Sampson Low, Marston, Searle and Rivington, 1884), preface

8   G. B. Shaw, *Fabianism and the Empire: A Manifesto by the Fabian Society* (Grant Richards, 1900), pp. 23–4

9   G. E. Buckle, *The Life of Benjamin Disraeli, Earl of Beaconsfield* (John Murray, 1920), Vol. V, pp. 194–5, 196

10 *Speeches of Lord Curzon, Viceroy of India* (Government Printer, Calcutta, 1902)

11 G. E. Buckle, ed., *The Letters of Queen Victoria* (John Murray, 1928), Second Series, Vol. III, pp. 447 and 451

12 J. Inglis ('Maori'), *Sport and Work on the Nepaul Frontier*, (Macmillan, 1878), pp. 154–5

13 J. A. Hobson, *The Psychology of Jingoism* (Grant Richards, 1901), pp. 2–3, 8–9

14 *The Times*, March 2nd, 1893

15 *The Nineteenth Century*, September 1895, pp. 449–50 and 450–51

16 S. Gwynn, *The Life of Mary Kingsley* (Macmillan, 1932), p. 121

17 Joseph Chamberlain, *Foreign and Colonial Speeches* (Routledge and Sons, 1897), pp. 130–33

18 V. I. Lenin, *Imperialism* (Moscow ed., 1934), p. 76

19 J. A. Hobson, *Imperialism* (James Nisbet, 1902), pp. 98–9

20 Rudyard Kipling, 'On the City Wall', *Soldiers Three and Other Stories* (Macmillan, 1907), pp. 323–4

21 C. Headlam, ed., *The Milner Papers* (Cassell, 1931), Vol. I, pp. 105–6

22 *The Nation and Athenaeum*, May 23rd, 1925 (*New Statesman*)

23 David Livingstone, *Expedition to the Zambesi and Its Tributaries* ('The Popular Account', John Murray, 1875) pp. 95–6, 141

24 Gertrude Ward, ed. *Letters of Bishop Tozer* (Universities Mission to Central Africa, 1902), p. 86

25 Gwynn, p. 126
26 J. G. Paton, in *Parliamentary Papers*, Vol. XLVII, 1883 (C 3814), pp. 29–30
27 Colonial Office Letter, May 16th, 1889, P.R.O. CO 879/30, p 71
28 E. Hertslet, *The Map of Africa by Treaty* (H.M.S.O. 1909), Vol. i, pp. 150–1
29 F. Weld, Dispatch to Colonial Office from Singapore, October 21st, 1880, P.R.O. CO 273/104, pp. 556–66
30 G. Townsend Warner, *A Brief Survey of British History* (Blackie, c. 1901), pp. 247–8
31 The *Daily News*, December 12th, 1866
32 G. Parkin, *Imperial Federation* (Macmillan, 1892), pp. 31–4, 37–8, 50–51, 56–7
33 E. A. Freeman, *Greater Greece and Greater Britain* (Macmillan, 1886), pp. 136–8
34 R. Jebb, *The Imperial Conference* (Longmans, 1911), Vol. I, pp. 17–18
35 *Hansard: Parliamentary Debates*, 4th Series, Vol. 83: 46, 47, 55, 56
36 *Hansard*, 4th Series, Vol. 83: 103
37 *Hansard*, 3rd Series, Vol. 227: 660–61
38 Parliamentary Papers, Vol. XLIV, 1903 (C 1597), pp. 5–8
39 R. Jebb, *Studies in Colonial Nationalism* (Edward Arnold, 1903), pp. 208–9

(Some of these documents were first noticed by us in print by citation or by their place in collections of documents. As far as possible we have gone to the originals in print or in manuscript. The exceptions are Nos. 2, 16, 18, 25, 34 and 39.)

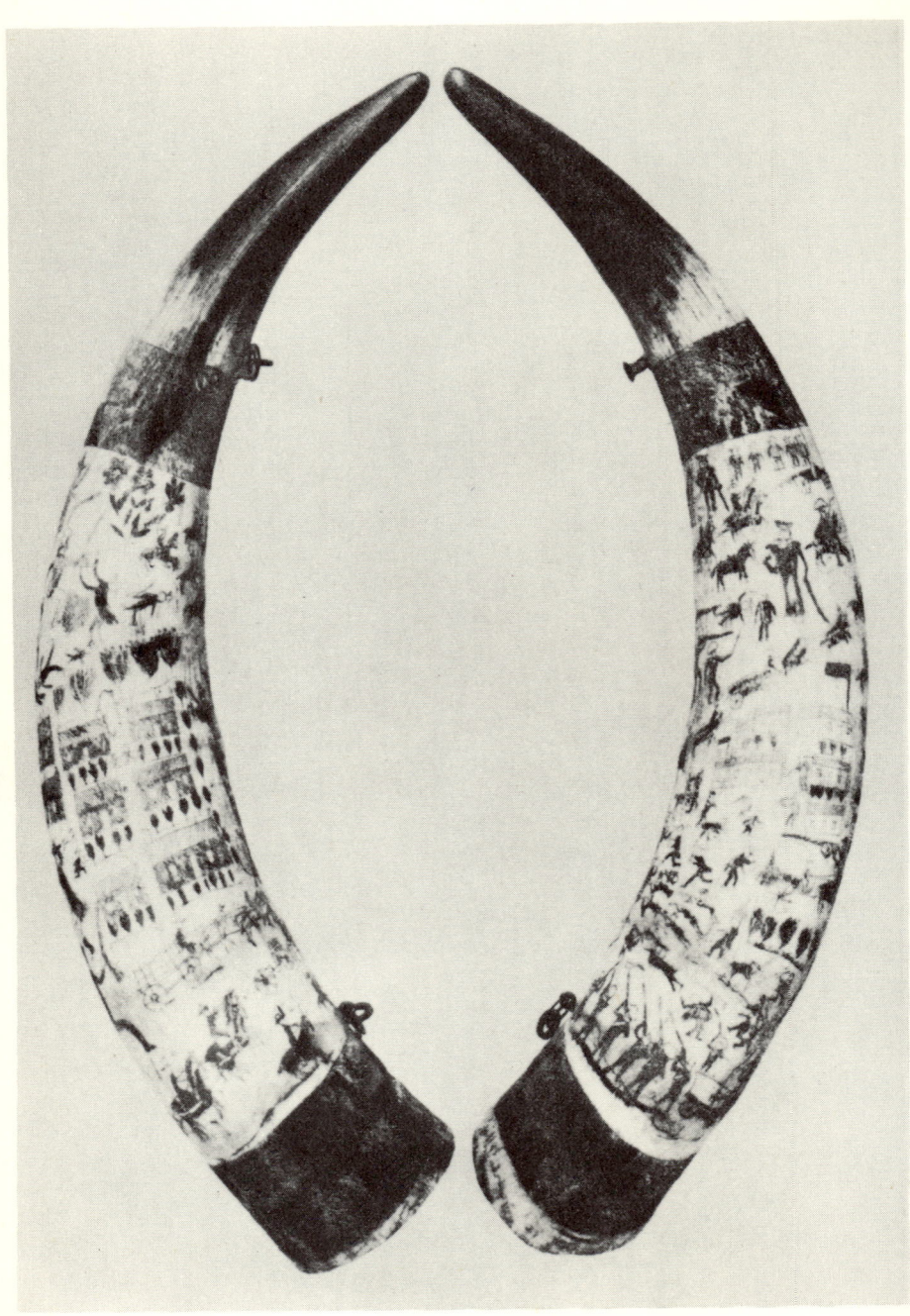

A history of the South African war, depicted by a native of the
Bedford District, Cape Colony.